WELCOME TO MY COUNTRY

Welcome to
PANAMA

Gareth Stevens Publishing
A WORLD ALMANAC EDUCATION GROUP COMPANY

Written by
RONALD TAN

Edited by
KATHARINE BROWN-CARPENTER

Edited in USA by
JENETTE DONOVAN GUNTLY

Designed by
BENSON TAN

Picture research by
THOMAS KHOO
JOSHUA ANG

First published in North America in 2006 by
Gareth Stevens Publishing
A WRC Media Company
330 West Olive Street, Suite 100
Milwaukee, Wisconsin 53212 USA

Please visit our web site at
www.garethstevens.com
For a free color catalog describing
Gareth Stevens Publishing's list of high-quality
books and multimedia programs,
call 1-800-542-2595 (USA) or
1-800-387-3178 (Canada).
Gareth Stevens Publishing's fax: (414) 332-3567.

© **MARSHALL CAVENDISH INTERNATIONAL (ASIA)
PRIVATE LIMITED 2005**
Originated and designed by
Times Editions—Marshall Cavendish
An imprint of Marshall Cavendish International (Asia) Pte Ltd
A member of Times Publishing Limited
Times Centre, 1 New Industrial Road
Singapore 536196
http://www.marshallcavendish.com/genref

Library of Congress Cataloging-in-Publication Data
Tan, Ronald.
Welcome to Panama / Ronald Tan.
p. cm. — (Welcome to my country)
Includes bibliographical references and index.
ISBN 0-8368-3135-7 (lib. bdg.)
1. Panama — Juvenile literature. I. Title. II. Series.
F1563.2.T36   2005
972.87—dc22   2005042558

Printed in Singapore

1 2 3 4 5 6 7 8 9 09 08 07 06 05

PICTURE CREDITS
Agence France Presse: 36, 38 (both), 39
Art Directors & TRIP Photo Library:
  3 (center), 6, 8, 12, 14, 18, 32, 34
Camera Press: 15 (bottom), 29, 30, 31
CORBIS: 13, 16
Corel: 3 (bottom)
Focus Team—Italy: 1, 28, 33, 40, 41
Robert Francis/Hutchison Picture Library: 2
Dr. Jon Fuller/Hutchison Picture Library:
  9 (top), 10 (top), 26
Getty Images/Hulton Archive: 11,
  15 (top and center)
James Davis Travel Photography: cover,
  4, 24
Life File Photo Library: 19
Lonely Planet Images: 5, 9 (bottom), 37
Tan Chung Lee: 45
Topham Picturepoint: 3 (top), 7, 17, 20, 21,
  22, 23, 25, 35
Travel Ink Photo and Feature Library:
  10 (bottom), 27

Digital Scanning by Superskill Graphics Pte Ltd

Contents

Words that appear in the glossary are printed in **boldface** type the first time they occur in the text.

Welcome to Panama!

The **Republic** of Panama is located between the North and South American **continents.** Panama is an important place to trade goods. Since 1914, ships have been able to travel between the Atlantic and Pacific Oceans through the Panama Canal. Let's explore Panama and learn about its friendly people!

Opposite: The Bridge of the Americas links the two halves of Panama as well as the continents of North and South America. It was completed in 1962.

Below: Panamanian girls play at a water pump in a village in the **province** of Bocas del Toro.

The Flag of Panama

Panama's flag has four rectangles with one blue and one red star on the white rectangles. Blue and red stand for the two main political parties when Panama became **independent**. White is for peace between the two parties.

The Land

Panama is on an **isthmus** that connects North and South America. The country has a land area of 29,332 square miles (75,990 square kilometers). To the west of Panama is Costa Rica. Colombia is to the east. The Caribbean Sea, which is part of the Atlantic Ocean, is north of Panama. The Pacific Ocean is to the south. The Gulf of Panama, to the south of Panama, is part of the Pacific Ocean.

Below: Coronado Beach is just one of Panama's many beautiful beaches. It is located on the Pacific coast west of Panama City, which is the capital city of Panama.

Barú Volcano, the country's highest point, stands 11,400 feet (3,475 meters) high. It is located between the Tabasará Mountains and the Talamanca Range in the west. In the east are the Darién Mountains, Sapo Mountains, Cordillera de San Blas, and Majé Mountains.

Many islands are part of Panama. Parida Island, Coiba Island, and Cébaco Island are off the Pacific coast. Off the Caribbean coast are the Bocas del Toro **Archipelago** and the San Blas Islands.

Above: In 1998, the water level of the Chagres River ran low because of too little rain. The Chagres and Tuira Rivers are two of Panama's more important rivers.

Climate

Panama has three main climate types. Most of the country is on low land that is hot and **humid**. Temperatures rarely fall below 79° Fahrenheit (26° Celsius) in most areas of Panama. Small regions of Panama are higher up and have mild weather. A few regions in Panama are high enough to be cold.

Panama has a rainy and a dry season, but the seasons are different in different areas of the nation. Panama's Caribbean coast may receive as much as 50 inches (1,270 millimeters) more rain than the Pacific coast during the rainy season.

Left: Northern Panama gets heavy rain during the rainy season. The rainfall helps the region's **tropical** forests stay green and healthy.

Left: Peanut-head bugs can be found in the rain forests of Panama. The bugs belong to the Fulgorid family of insects. Most peanut-head bugs reach a length of about 3 inches (8 centimeters).

Plants and Animals

Tropical rain forests grow in the wet northern regions of Panama. Trees such as wild cashew and rubber trees grow in the rain forests. **Savannas** cover much of drier southern Panama. In areas with a mild climate, **montane** forests grow. Orchids grow in many areas of Panama.

Panama has many kinds of animals, including jaguars, tapirs, and anteaters. Animals such as giant sea turtles live in the oceans around Panama. Nearly 950 kinds of birds also live in Panama.

Below: The Strawberry Poison Dart frog is found only in Nicaragua, Costa Rica, and Panama. The frog can grow to a length of about 1.25 inches (3 cm).

History

Scientists believe people lived in what is now Panama as early as 10,000 B.C. These early settlers hunted and fished. By 5000 B.C., the settlers were growing crops such as corn.

By 2800 B.C., the people of present-day Panama were making pottery. By A.D. 500, the early people were making stone sculptures. They also made crafts from gold or carved shells and bones. These early settlers were the **ancestors** of the American Indian groups, such as the Chocó and Kuna, in Panama today.

Above: This is an example of pottery made by the early settlers of what is now Panama. Each of the hollow legs holds a ball that rolls up and down.

Left: Many people believe that the drawings on this rock in the Chiriquí province were made by American Indians hundreds of years ago.

The Spanish Arrive

In 1501, the Spanish arrived in what is now Panama. The Spanish tried to set up **colonies**, but American Indians in the region fought them. Finally, Vasco Núñez de Balboa set up a colony called Santa María de la Antigua del Darién. In 1519, Pedro Arias de Ávila became **governor**. His rule was harsh. That same year, the people of Santa María moved to a new town called Panama.

Rule of the Spanish

In the early 1500s, the town of Panama became an important center of trade for the Spanish. In 1538, the Spanish gave Panama some independence. Panama grew, as did many towns nearby.

In 1671, a Welsh pirate named Henry Morgan led an attack on Panama and destroyed the town. Panama was rebuilt in 1673, but it was not as important as it had been. In 1739, Panama lost its independence. The town and much of northern South America became part of New Granada, a Spanish colony.

Left: During the 1600s and 1700s, the Spanish built many forts in the town of Portobelo. The forts protected their ships, which were loaded with treasure taken from all over the region. Many of the forts still stand today.

Left: A large ship passes through the Panama Canal on its way to the Pacific Ocean. The canal was officially opened in 1914. It is about 40 miles (65 kilometers) long.

In the early 1800s, many Spanish-ruled lands in the Americas fought for their independence. In 1821, Panama gained its freedom and joined Gran Colombia, which included present-day Colombia, Venezuela, and Ecuador.

After a new **constitution** was passed in 1843, Panama became a state in Colombia. On November 3, 1903, with support from the United States, Panama declared its independence. In 1904, the United States was given control of the Canal Zone, the area of land that would become the site of the Panama Canal.

Left: Manuel Antonio Noriega Morena (*front, far right*) ruled Panama from 1983 to 1989. His rule was harsh and dishonest. In 1984, he fixed the results of elections so that he would win. He also had people who fought against him killed.

Toward Democracy

Panama was a **democracy** from 1903 to 1968. In 1968, Colonel Omar Torrijos Herrera took control. Even though he ruled as a **dictator**, Torrijos was still a popular leader. In the 1970s, he made the United States agree to turn over control of the Panama Canal to Panama in 1999. Torrijos died in 1981, and in 1983, Colonel Manuel Antonio Noriega Morena took control. He also ruled as a dictator. In 1989, the United States sent troops to take control of Panama. They helped Panama return to a democracy.

Vasco Núñez de Balboa (1475–1519)

Spanish explorer Vasco Núñez de Balboa was the first European to see the Pacific Ocean from the isthmus. In 1513, Balboa and his crew crossed the land separating Panama's Caribbean and Pacific coasts in twenty-four days.

Vasco Núñez de Balboa

Ferdinand de Lesseps (1805–1894)

Ferdinand de Lesseps was the first person to try to build the Panama Canal. Digging the canal was hard work. The workers also suffered from diseases and the hot climate. These problems forced de Lesseps to give up the canal project.

Ferdinand de Lesseps

Mireya Elisa Moscoso Rodriguez (1946–)

Mireya Elisa Moscoso Rodriguez helped set up a political party called the Arnulfista Party in 1990. In 1999, Moscoso became Panama's first female president. She is the widow of former president Arnulfo Arias Madrid.

Mireya Elisa Moscoso Rodriguez

Government and the Economy

The government of Panama has three branches. The president and two vice presidents head the executive branch. They make rules for the government and also lead it. The president and vice presidents can serve only one five-year term. The legislative, or lawmaking, branch is a **parliament**. It is called the Legislative Assembly. Its members may serve more than one five-year term.

Below: The Panama National Assembly Building in Panama City is where members of the Legislative Assembly gather to make laws.

Panama's judicial branch is headed by the Supreme Court of Justice. The court oversees Panama's lower courts. The nine judges in the Supreme Court of Justice serve ten-year terms.

Local Government

Panama is divided into nine provinces and two *comarcas* (kow-MAHR-kahz). The comarcas are regions set aside for the country's American Indian groups. A **tribal** leader heads each comarca. A governor heads each province.

Above: The presidential guards help keep law and order in Panama. Since 1990, Panama has made it against the law to form an army. Instead, the country depends on forces such as the presidential guards to keep the peace.

The Economy

Since the time of Spanish rule, Panama has been an important place for trade. After the Panama Canal was opened in 1914, the country became even more important to shipping companies from around the world. The Panama Canal is Panama's largest employer. More than half of all Panamanians work in service industries. Most service jobs are located along the canal. Banking and tourism are also important service industries.

Left: Panamanian men unload boxes of bananas from a truck. In Panama, many people do not have job skills. The lack of skills makes it hard for many people to find jobs.

Farming and Industries

Some Panamanians work in farming. Crops grown in Panama include rice, bananas, corn, coffee, sugarcane, and vegetables. Many farm products are **exported**. Seafood caught in the oceans surrounding Panama is also exported.

Panama has several industries, such as making sugar, cement, and clothing. Other Panamanian industries include making products from oil and making construction materials.

Above: The National Bank of Panama is located in Panama City. It is the country's main bank.

People and Lifestyle

Most people in Panama are *mestizos* (mays-TEE-sohs), people who have a mixture of European and American Indian ancestors. Some Panamanians have West Indian ancestors, ancestors who were both African and American Indian. A small number of people in Panama have only European ancestors. Panama also has some small Arab and Chinese communities.

Below:
These people in Panama have West Indian ancestors. More than half of Panamanians are between the ages of fifteen and sixty-four. Almost one-third of the people are fourteen years old or younger.

City and Country Life

Many Panamanians live in cities near the Panama Canal, including the cities of San Miguelito, Colón, La Chorrera, Cristóbal, and Panama City. Panama City is Panama's most important center of industry, trade, politics, and **culture**.

Most **rural** Panamanians live on the plains and low hills between the Azuero Peninsula and the Tabasará Mountains. Few people live in the mountain areas.

Above: Much of the city of Colón is run down because most of the people living there are very poor.

Health Care

In Panama, most people who have full-time jobs can go to a health center or hospital for free or at a low cost. The country has public and private health centers, but private care is expensive.

Most cities have at least one health care center. In the countryside, the most important health needs are clean water and sewer systems. Many rural areas in Panama do not have these basics, so the health of rural Panamanians suffers.

Below: In the 1980s, the government of Panama worked to make clean drinking water and sewer systems available in rural areas and in many of the poor, rundown areas of Panama's cities.

HIV/AIDS in Panama

In 2003, about 16,000 Panamanians were living with HIV, which is the **virus** that leads to the disease called AIDS. About five hundred people died of AIDS that year. Panama held a meeting in 2003 to talk about the best ways to treat people with the disease. The government is also working with international groups to help HIV/AIDS patients get medical care and to educate Panamanians about the disease.

Above: This man does not have a job, and he lives in an old, empty train car. Because he does not have a job, he cannot get free health care at Panama's public health centers.

Education

In Panama, children must attend school between the ages of six and fifteen. Students attend primary, or elementary, school for six years. After they finish primary school, students attend general secondary, or high, school. It lasts for three years. Students may then choose to go on to academic secondary school. Academic secondary school lasts for three years and prepares students to attend a college or university.

Below: A group of Kuna American Indian children attends a primary school class. Most classes in Panama are taught in the Spanish language.

Higher Education

Panama has several universities. The oldest university in the country is the University of Panama. At a university, students may study subjects such as architecture, farming, law, or medicine.

Students in Panama may also choose from other schools of higher education, including teacher training colleges and **vocational** schools.

Above: In 2000, some University of Panama students blocked off a road outside the school. They were against the decision to allow the United States to open an antidrug center near the Panama Canal. The students felt the United States was just trying to keep U.S. soldiers in their country.

Religion

Panamanians are free to choose their own religions. The country does not have an official religion. Most people in Panama are Roman Catholics. Some Catholics in the nation go to church regularly, but many Catholics in cities do not. Most Panamanian Catholics do attend church on holidays, including Christmas and Easter, and for religious ceremonies, such as baptisms.

Left:
The Metropolitan Cathedral, which is in Panama City, is a Roman Catholic church. It took more than one hundred years to build. It is a good example of the style of architecture built when the Spanish ruled Panama.

Left: This is the Elmslie Memorial United Church. It is a Presbyterian church. Most of the Presbyterians in Panama live in the provinces of Colón and Panamá.

Protestant religions, including the Episcopalian, Seventh-Day Adventist, Mormon, Presbyterian, and Jehovah's Witness faiths, are growing in Panama.

Other Beliefs

Some Muslims, who are followers of the Islamic religion, live in Panama. Islam came to Panama in the mid-sixteenth century. Today, West Indians from neighboring countries, such as Jamaica, Trinidad, and Barbados, make up most of the nation's Muslims. Some Panamanians are also followers of the Baha'i, Jewish, and Hindu faiths.

Language

Spanish is Panama's official language. It is used in government, trade, and education. Many people in Panama also speak English, especially in business. Some Panamanians speak a language called pidgin English. It is a mixture of English and local languages. Panama has nine American Indian languages, including Buglere, Teribe, Woun Meu, Kuna, Emberá, and Ngäbere. A small number of people in Panama also speak Chinese languages or Arabic.

Left: This woman in Panama is reading a Spanish-language newspaper. After 1999, Panamanian newspapers were given more freedom to write about important people in the country. The government still tightly controls the media, however.

Literature

In the past, most of the literature read in Panama was written by people in other **Latin American** nations, such as Peru, Mexico, or Colombia. Panama became known for its own literature during the 1900s. Panama's most respected writer is probably Ricardo Miró (1883–1940). Miró is famous for his poetry. A prize for literature is named after him. Today, important Panamanian writers include Raúl Leis and Ariel Barria Alvarado.

Above:
Professor Carlos Fuentes (1928–) is a well-known Latin American author. He was born in Panama but has lived most of his life in Mexico. He is best known for his novel *La Region Mas Transparente*, or "Where the Air is Clear."

Arts

Music and Dance

Panamanian music combines African, American Indian, Spanish, Caribbean, and Latin American styles of music. Drums, bells, flutes, and castanets are popular instruments in Panama. Even though Panamanians enjoy listening to many styles of music, such as ska, salsa, tango, and reggae, folk music is a favorite in the country. Folk music in Panama is famous for its African drumbeats and Spanish singing styles.

Left:
Chocolate Genius is a Panamanian-born singer and songwriter who lives in the United States. His real name is Marc Anthony Thompson.

Panamanians also love to dance. The country's national dance is called *tamborito* (TAHM-boh-REE-toh), which means "little drum."

Panamanian Painters

Some Panamanian painters are famous throughout the world. Roberto Lewis (1874–1949) is well known for his **murals**. Humberto Ivaldi (1909–1947) became well known for his paintings, such as *Wind on the Hill* (1945). Today, Alfredo Sinclair (1915–) is a famous painter. He has held shows of his work in Panama and many other countries.

Crafts

American Indians in Panama make many kinds of crafts, such as baskets, pottery, **embroidery**, and wood carvings. The Wounaan and Emberá people are known for their hand-woven baskets and for sculptures carved on *tagua* (TAH-gwah) nuts. The people of La Peña are known for their colorful pottery. The pottery is made using American Indian styles from long ago.

Below: Pieces of *mola* (MOU-lah) stitch work hang on display. Kuna American Indian women are famous for mola, which is made by sewing many layers of cloth together to create colorful patterns.

People in different provinces of Panama are known for different crafts. In the 1900s, many pieces of pottery were found in the Coclé province. The pottery was decorated with shapes or with drawings of people and animals. People in the Herrara and Los Santos provinces are famous for making the *pollera* (pou-YEH-rah), the national dress of Panama. It consists of a ruffled top and a long skirt. Often, both parts have colorful embroidery.

Leisure

Panamanians enjoy spending free time with their families. Many people enjoy outdoor activities such as hiking and camping. Many Panamanians also like to visit local beaches, where they can sunbathe, surf, or swim.

Some Panamanians in cities spend weekends visiting their family members who live in the countryside. Often, people who stay in cities on weekends watch movies, dine out, or go shopping.

Below: Panamanian men often gather to play dominoes.

Family Time

At home, Panamanian families often have meals together so that they can discuss the day's events. Many families also watch television together to relax. Most households consist of parents and children. Some households also include grandparents. Single-parent families are also common in Panama. Panamanians often attend family celebrations, such as birthdays and weddings. Most events include music, dancing, and food.

Above:
In Panama, children enjoy playing in the water or in the sand at local beaches.

Sports

Baseball is the most popular sport in Panama. Many Panamanians spend a lot of time playing baseball and watching baseball games. More than forty people from Panama have played professional baseball in the United States, including Rod Carew, Bruce Chen, Einar Diaz, Mariano Rivera, and Carlos Lee.

Basketball is another favorite sport in Panama. The nation has regional teams and a national basketball team that has played in many important competitions.

Left:
The Panamanian national baseball team celebrates after beating Brazil. The two teams played in the 2002 Intercontinental Baseball Cup, which was held in Cuba.

Many Panamanians enjoy sports such as jogging, hunting, cycling, horseback riding, tennis, and fishing. Soccer has also become a popular sport in Panama. The nation has several soccer teams, including Panamá Viejo and Tauro.

Some Panamanians enjoy watching and betting on **cockfights** and horse races. Some people also enjoy watching bullfights, which are mainly held during festivals. In Panama, unlike in some other countries, the bulls are not killed during the bullfights.

Above:
These Panamanians are paddling along the Chagres River. Many Panamanians enjoy water sports, such as kayaking, swimming, diving, and snorkeling.

Left: On Good Friday, the Friday before Easter, some Roman Catholics in Panama act out Jesus Christ's trial and also act out Jesus being hung on the cross.

Religious Festivals

Many festivals in Panama are religious. One of the country's most important festivals is Carnival, a Roman Catholic festival. It is usually celebrated during the four days before Ash Wednesday. Carnival is a time of dancing, feasting, and parades with floats and costumes. Holy Week is important in Panama as well. It honors the days before Jesus Christ died and ends on Easter Sunday.

Below: Roman Catholic children carry crosses as they walk through Panama City on Good Friday.

National Holidays and Festivals

Panamanians celebrate many national holidays. On November 3, the country celebrates Panama's independence from Colombia. Independence from Spain is celebrated on November 28. Mother's Day falls on December 8.

Panama has many national festivals. Each September, the National Folkloric Festival of La Mejorana is held. The festival celebrates Panamanian life and customs with folk musical instruments, singing, dancing, and bullfighting.

Left: Panamanian schoolchildren wave their country's national flag during Independence Day celebrations on November 3.

Food

Food in Panama has been influenced by American Indian, Spanish, and African cooking styles. Most meals include rice, legumes, beans, corn, yams, **cassava**, or plantains, which are similar to bananas. One favorite dish is *sancocho* (sahn-KOH-shoh). It is chicken and vegetable soup. *Tamales* (tah-MAHL-ehs) are pieces of cornmeal dough stuffed with chicken or pork and vegetables, then wrapped in banana leaves.

Left:
Dishes made from crayfish (*center, bottom*) and grilled fish (*far right*) are commonly served at restaurants in Panama. Most people in Panama eat lots of seafood.

As a side dish, many Panamanians enjoy plantains cooked in butter and sugar. The dish is topped with nutmeg, cinnamon, or cheese. *Arroz con guando* (ah-ROHS con GUAN-doh) is also a favorite side dish. It is made from rice and beans cooked in coconut milk.

Panamanians also enjoy snacks, such as fried plantains. *Hojaldras* (ou-HAHL-drahs), a flat piece of fried dough, is often eaten as a snack or for breakfast.

Favorite drinks in Panama include *chichas* (CHEE-chas), which are fruit juices mixed with water and sugar.

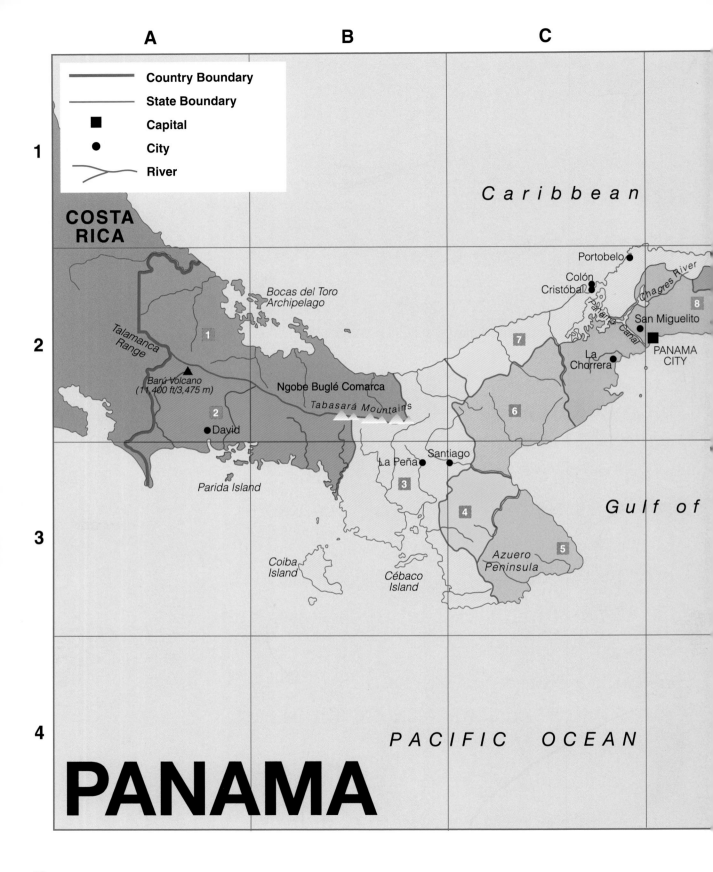

A   B   C

1

2

3

4

COSTA
RICA

Caribbean

Portobelo

Colón
Cristóbal

Chagres River

San Miguelito

Talamanca
Range

Barú Volcano
(11,400 ft/3,475 m)

*Bocas del Toro
Archipelago*

1

Panama Canal

8

La
Chorrera

PANAMA
CITY

Ngobe Buglé Comarca

7

6

2

David

Tabasará Mountains

Parida Island

La Peña

Santiago

3

4

*Coiba
Island*

*Cébaco
Island*

*Azuero
Peninsula*

5

Gulf of

PACIFIC OCEAN

PANAMA

Legend:
— Country Boundary
— State Boundary
■ Capital
● City
〰 River

42

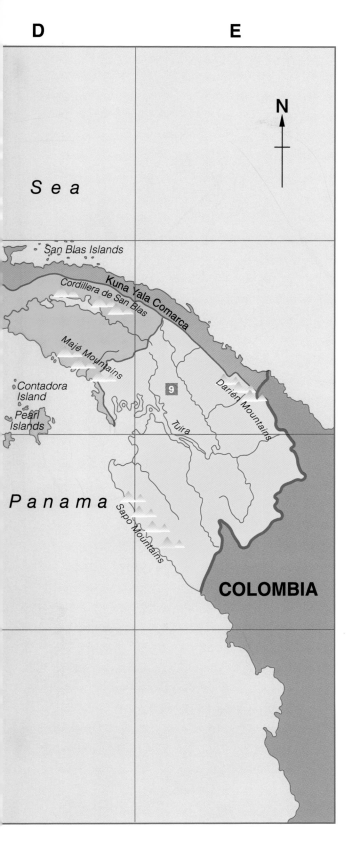

D   **E**

N

S e a

San Blas Islands

Kuna Yala Comarca

Cordillera de San Blas

Majé Mountains

Contadora Island

Pearl Islands

Darién Mountains

Tuira

9

P a n a m a

Sapo Mountains

COLOMBIA

PROVINCES

1 **Bocas del Toro**
2 **Chiriquí**
3 **Veraguas**
4 **Herrera**
5 **Los Santos**
6 **Coclé**
7 **Colón**
8 **Panamá**
9 **Darién**

Azuero Peninsula C3

Barú Volcano A2
Bocas del Toro Archipelago A2–B2

Caribbean Sea A1–E2
Cébaco Island B3
Chagres River C2–D2
Coiba Island B3
Colombia E2–E4
Colón (city) C2
Contadora Island D2
Cordillera de San Blas D2–E2
Costa Rica A1–A3
Cristóbal (city) C2

Darién Mountains E2–E3
David A2

Gulf of Panama C2–E3

Kuna Yala Comarca D2–E2

La Chorrera (city) C2
La Peña (city) B3

Majé Mountains D2

Ngobe Buglé Comarca B3

Pacific Ocean A2–E4
Panama Canal C2
Panama City D2
Parida Island A3
Pearl Islands D2–D3
Portobelo (city) C2

San Blas Islands D2
San Miguelito (city) C2
Santiago C3
Sapo Mountains D3–E3

Tabasará Mountains B2
Talamanca Range A2
Tuira River E2–E3

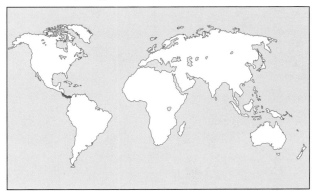

Quick Facts

Official Name	Republic of Panama
Capital	Panama City
Official Language	Spanish
Population	3,000,463 (July 2004 estimate)
Land Area	29,332 square miles (75,990 square km)
Provinces	Bocas del Toro, Chiriquí, Coclé, Colón, Darién, Herrera, Los Santos, Panamá, Veraguas
Comarcas	Kuna Yala, Ngobe Buglé
Major Cities	Panama City, Cólon, David, Santiago
Highest Point	Barú Volcano 11,400 feet (3,475 m)
Main Religion	Roman Catholicism
Major Rivers	Chagres, Tuira
Famous Leaders	Manuel Amador Guerrero (1833–1909)
	Omar Torrijos Herrera (1929–1981)
	Manuel Antonio Noriega Morena (1938–)
	Mireya Elisa Moscoso Rodriguez (1946–)
Currency	Balboa (PAB 1 = U.S. $1 as of 2005) Note: U.S. dollars are legal tender in Panama.

Opposite: A Kuna American Indian woman sits in front of her display of mola stitch work while she waits for customers.

Glossary

ancestors: family members from the past, farther back than grandparents.

archipelago: a chain of islands.

cassava: a root also known as tapioca.

cockfights: contests in which two roosters are put in a pen to fight.

colonies: villages set up in countries and controlled by other countries.

constitution: a set of citizen rights and laws for a country's government.

continents: Earth's main landmasses, including North and South America.

culture: the customs, beliefs, language, and arts of one group or country.

democracy: a government in which citizens elect their leaders by vote.

dictator: a ruler who keeps complete control of a country, often by force.

embroidery: the art of decorating cloth or clothes with fancy sewing.

exported (v): sold and shipped from one country to another country.

governor: a person who is elected to be the head of a region or state.

humid: damp; usually meaning the amount of water in the air.

independent: regarding being free of control by others.

isthmus: a narrow piece of land that has water on both sides and that connects two larger pieces of land.

Latin American: regarding areas in the Americas south of the United States.

montane: relating to or growing on the high slopes of a mountain.

murals: large pictures painted directly onto walls or ceilings.

parliament: a government group that makes the laws for their country.

province: a region of a country with set borders and its own local officials.

republic: a country in which citizens elect their own lawmakers.

rural: relating to the countryside.

savannas: dry grasslands.

tribal: relating to tribes, people from the same family, nation, or race.

tropical: relating to very warm and wet regions where plants grow all year.

virus: an infection that causes diseases.

vocational: relating to a job, profession, or skilled trade.

More Books to Read

Henry Morgan: Seventeenth-Century Buccaneer. Library of Pirates series. Aileen Weintraub (PowerKids Press)

Into the Sea. Brenda Z. Guiberson (Henry Holt)

Into Wild Panama. The Jeff Corwin Experience series. Ed. Elaine Pascoe (Blackbirch Press)

Life at the Top: Discoveries in a Tropical Forest Canopy. Rain Forest Pilot series. Ellen Doris (Raintree Steck-Vaughn)

Mola: Cuna Life Stories and Art. Maricel E. Presilla (Henry Holt)

Panama. Countries of the World series. Marc Tyler Nobleman (Bridgestone Books)

The Panama Canal. Wonders of the World series. Elizabeth Mann (Mikaya Press)

Vasco Núñez de Balboa: Explorer to the Pacific Ocean. Explorers! series. Arlene Bourgeois Molzahn (Enslow Publishers)

Videos

Geography of Mexico and Central America. (Discovery Channel)

National Geographic: Panama Wild: Rain Forest of Life. (Questar)

The Panama Canal. (Superior Promotions)

Web Sites

striweb.si.edu/forest_speaks/en/index2.htm

www.enchantedlearning.com/explorers/page/b/balboa.shtml

www.pancanal.com/eng/general/howitworks/

Due to the dynamic nature of the Internet, some web sites stay current longer than others. To find additional web sites, use a reliable search engine with one or more of the following keywords to help you locate information about Panama. Keywords: *Vasco Balboa, mola, Panama Canal, peanut-head bug, tapir.*

Index